How
TO
Heal
Your
Soul

Written By

Max Samn

Max Samn

No part of this publication might be imitated, dispersed, or transmitted in any shape using any and all means, including photocopying, recording, or other electronic or mechanical techniques, without the prior written authorization of the publisher.

ISBN: 9781720177302

Content

Introduction

I am so tired of all the cynicism around me! It is safe to say that you are? This world is lethal and it is debilitated. I detest viewing the news, perusing the daily paper or notwithstanding collaborating with my neighbors. I would prefer not to seem solitary. I really love individuals. Be that as it may, this world has made us chilly and coldblooded.

The outcome is a general public of miserable individuals. Well more than half of all relational unions end in separate. Well, more than half of every single youthful grown-up don't have faith in marriage. We have to return to the days where it was anything but difficult to converse with outsiders and it was unnatural not to be well mannered.

Back to the days where individuals really trusted in affection and looked out for their neighbors. We have to begin adoring ourselves once more. We each should be the change we wish to find on the planet. We have to mend ourselves and begin adoring ourselves once more.

Upbeat individuals are effective individuals. This is essentially in light of the fact that being cheerful makes it simple to remain persuaded to achieving your objectives. Your considerations have an exceptionally noteworthy effect on the existence you lead and the nature of the connections you will have with relatives, companions, and hug others. Some even reason that our contemplations and convictions can have a much more grounded impact on our wellbeing than present-day pharmaceutical. Think about these illustrations:

- A moderately aged man kicks the bucket multi-day after his Doctor determined him to have Cancer, despite the fact that his post-mortem examination uncovered he was misdiagnosed.

- Many ladies who are urgent to have a tyke will start to have genuine indications of a pregnancy, for example, longings and an expansion in the extent of their bosoms, in spite of the way that they are not really pregnant.

- People who experience the ill effects of Depression who take an interest in clinical preliminaries for new antidepressants begin encountering a change in their states of mind despite the fact that they were given the fake treatment and not the real medication.

That being stated, it has been deductively demonstrated that you can enhance your wellbeing, profession, and connections essentially by enhancing the manner in which you consider yourself and your general surroundings. This is a great deal less expensive than paying for sessions with a specialist or paying a Divorce Lawyer.

This book is proposed to enable you to mend yourself of the considerable number of scars and the impact of all the pessimism around. I ensure that figuring out how to free yourself from the agony of this world will radically enhance the nature of your life starting now and into the foreseeable future.

Section one - Act naturally

We as a whole need to figure out how to act naturally once more. This is a standout amongst the most urgent parts of effectively exploring through this fiasco we call life. This support is not the slightest bit giving you the privilege to be a yank. We have just talked about that mending ourselves from the torment caused by this world necessitates that we endeavor to dispose of our negative characteristics.

Characteristics, for example, being presumptuous, inconsiderate, untrustworthy and parsimonious have no place in your life. When we gladly stroll around with these appalling propensities, we are welcoming a wide range of cynicism into our lives. The consequence of that is just more torment and disillusionment. That is the reason I energized you in the plain first section to become more acquainted with yourself. This will better prepare you to mend yourself, by adapting more about your shortcomings.

So what precisely does it intend to act naturally? It necessitates that you separate yourself from every one of the marks our general surroundings has forced on us. These appalling marks come to fruition on account of the way

we look, the manner in which we dress or even the network we experienced childhood in. There is no explanation behind us to enable our general surroundings to press us into a form that doesn't generally speak to our identity. Simply consider how freeing it would be to not need to put on a show to be something you are most certainly not. This is all inside reason obviously. We could never need to take certain freedoms that may have broad impacts on our own lives, and may even endanger our occupations. That implies that you should need to hold off on anything uncommon, such as passing on your hair purple and green, to the point that you discover a business that will suit such a decision.

Here are 5 essential reasons why you have to begin being consistent with yourself:

1- You will never have the capacity to please everybody. On the off chance that you continually enable the general population around you to figure out your identity, you will always need to change a big motivator for you with a specific end goal to attempt and make everybody glad. The main issue with this is you will manage such huge numbers of clashing requests that you will, in the end, wind up frustrating somebody. Also, putting yourself under this sort of weight will abandon you feeling disappointed at last.

2- The society around us truly doesn't recognize what it needs. The media depicts both the resigned homemaker and the wild hard worker, as the perfect lady. Society additionally requests that men be delicate to the requirements of the contrary sex and the risky terrible kid also. Which will you be in the event that you are just permitting people around you to figure out your identity? Whatever you choose to be, simply recall that it is very debilitating to put on this sort of demonstrate each day.

3- You will wind up settling on groundbreaking choices in view of the impulses of the general population around you, who won't endure the results of these decisions. On the off chance that you choose to have a youngster, basically on the grounds that your family believes now is the right time, you will be the one to need to deal with that kid! In the event that you choose to seek after a vocation in light of the fact that your companions figure you would do well in it, you should live with the weight of a profession that you loathe, until the end of time.

4- The truth dependably turns out. At some point or another, individuals will start to understand that you are faking. Lamentably, as we find on account of numerous big names, reality frequently turns out in a major embarrassment or breakdown.

5- When you are content with your identity, you will be genuinely cheerful. How might you cherish yourself, when you are continually professing to be something that you are most certainly not?

At the point when all is said and done, you have to take control of your life on the off chance that you need to see genuine changes. You can't expect diverse outcomes in the event that you are not sufficiently strong to roll out extraordinary improvements. What's more, the ideal opportunity for those progressions is currently!

Section two - Be Generous

A generous individual isn't required to give every one of their belonging ceaselessly. A generous individual is additionally not required to enable others to drive them around. Being generous includes right off the bat, the preparation to give or be willing to give more than is required.

Being generous takes consideration to the following level. You may be caring on a basic level, and regularly consider helping other people, yet except if you really set aside the opportunity to really get this show on the road in offering your chance, vitality or different assets for the advantage of another individual, you have not genuinely aced the craft of being generous. Liberality moves us to give of ourselves readily, and expect nothing consequently.

I know you ought to think about how giving without end your advantages can enable you to carry on with a superior life. Actually numerous frequently respect liberality of one of the keys to being genuinely upbeat in this hopeless world. Actually, numerous restorative experts will verify the way that being generous is likewise useful for your wellbeing. Truth be told, here is a portion of the demonstrated advantages of giving generously:

- Reduced stretch

- Lessening the probability of agony from despondency

- Increased feeling of reason

- Greater bliss

- Stronger families and relational unions

- Less mess

- Reduced danger of dementia

- Greater thankfulness for everything that you have

- More liable to profit by the liberality of others

A generous individual frequently searches out chances to do useful for others. Simply consider volunteers who advance toward assist at Soup Kitchens consistently. Those of us overcome enough to agree to accept the Peace Corps are additionally considered very generous. Be that as it may, basically helping an elderly woman with her basic need sacks, or halting to enable a kid to cross the street, can be viewed as generous. This sort of worry for others demonstrates gainful in light of the fact that it compels us to center around the requirements of others rather than all alone issues. Anything that limits the impact of our issues, regardless of whether in our connections or even fiscally, will directly affect our well being. Being generous shields us from all the criticism and narcissism that makes it so difficult to explore our way through this world.

I would, nonetheless, urge you to be mindful as you try to be more generous. Be exceptionally watchful of the manner by which you show your liberality. If you don't mind be particularly watchful while being generous to individuals from the contrary sex. In the event that you are as of now taken, and you would prefer not to send the wrong impression, evade blessings or favors that are close to home in nature. An individual blessing is anything identified with one's body. Aroma, for instance, would be viewed as an individual blessing.

If it's not too much trouble likewise remember that your own well being may become possibly the most important factor while being generous. Numerous individuals have gotten ransacked when asked by an apparently vagrant to give some cash. Venturing into your wallet or sack, and uncovering where your money is kept, and how much money you have, is a terrible thought, regardless of how destitute the individual may give off an impression of being. A more secure choice is told the individual that you will come back with a blessing.

I would firmly propose that you go to a safe area, one that is far from prying eyes and bundle everything that you might want to give to this person ahead of time. My last expression of alert is that you have to get a handle on the individual before being excessively generous. A few people like suddenness and others incline toward on the off chance that you initially inquire as to whether they require your assistance. Indeed, even the best of expectations.

Section three - Be Tolerant

It is difficult to be tolerant. The simple presence of the need to utilize the word suggests that we have been harmed somehow. Tolerant a complaint, regardless of whether genuine or envisioned, will be extraordinary compared to other blessings you can give yourself. This is so whether you trust the individual merits such benevolence or not. When we decline to excuse, we end up angry. Clutching disdain resembles drinking poison, and expecting the person that wronged us to endure. It can likewise be contrasted with causing wounds without anyone else bodies, and anticipating that another person should feel the torment.

This rationale isn't just filled with blemishes, it is additionally very hazardous. Disdain can without much of a stretch progress toward becoming contempt and scorn is a monstrous thing. Yet, for what reason do we discover it so difficult to tolerant? On the off chance that easy-going somebody who hurt us will be so painful, for what reason does the specific thought of relinquishing the hurt influence us to feel so uneasy?

The genuine issue lies in the way that none of us need to keep remembering the repulsiveness of whatever wrong was done to us. Be that as it may, as we keep on thinking about how seriously we were harmed, we unknowingly start to consider making the individual pay for what they did. Our imperfect feeling of equity regularly constrains us to trust that on the off chance that we clutch all the torment that was caused and decline to release it, we will get the equity we merit.

This is particularly so when the individual does not have all the earmarks of being sad for what they have done. Sadly, we can't constrain the person to improve as a man by angrily withholding our fellowship or consideration from them. We are just harming ourselves as we drive our brains to remember the agony again and again.

While we are irately raging through existence with the greatness of disdain in our souls, our face, our discourse, and our state of mind will be antagonistically influenced.

Regardless of the way that we may have been wronged by one or perhaps a couple of people, everybody around us will start to be influenced. Disdain frequently makes us be touchy, discouraged, and by and large extremely repulsive. Also, to exacerbate the situation, usually our loved ones and not the general population that wronged us, who will wind up anguish because of what occurred.

The heaviness of disdain has additionally been known to influence our memory, efficiency at work, capacity to perform routine assignments, the capacity to center, and even our sex drive. Being intense, and declining to tolerant has likewise been connected to debilitated invulnerable frameworks, poor heart wellbeing, and even hypertension. As should be obvious, declining to excuse will never demonstrate usefully.

Be that as it may, what precisely is tolerant? Is it just overlooking what occurred? Does tolerant imply we essentially imagine that nothing happened? Not a chance. It isn't that straightforward. When we excuse, we should include more than our words.

We should change how we contemplate the person. It seems as though we are enabling them to begin with a fresh start once more. You decline to enable the circumstance to cause you or the gatherings required to hurt you anymore. This requires an abnormal state of passionate knowledge, poise, and love. Tolerant isn't simply "letting them free" for what they did, it is enabling those included to quit choosing not to move on and proceed onward to more essential things.

Turning into that goaded because of another person's activities, and enabling yourself to stay annoyed with what occurred for an expanded timeframe, is extremely giving the individual they keys to your satisfaction. It seems as though you are enabling that person to control you, and they will keep on controlling you until the point when you gather up the strength expected to excuse them.

Tolerant is likewise advantageous on the grounds that it regularly results when we end up mindful of our own deficiencies. It ends up simpler for us to excuse when we recollect that we too have needed to request tolerant commonly. In opposition to what we may trust, we are not great. We here and there hurt the general population around us, even the ones we adore, without acknowledging it. When we decline to harbor disdain and practice absolution, it will be simple for people around us to excuse us when we blunder.

Here are a couple of reasons why it is helpful to work on being excusing:

- You will be a considerable measure more joyful and in a vastly improved state of mind.
- You will rest better around evening time.
- You won't risk your activity by not being profitable.
- You won't risk your association with your better half or your family.
- You will learn more noteworthy discretion and mindfulness.
- You will appreciate more noteworthy peace.
- You will pick up the regard of everyone around you.
- You will never again feel the torment of the harm that was finished.
- You will encounter less uneasiness.
- Your confidence will increment as you watch your very own quality.

What Forgiveness isn't!

Being tolerant does not mean you must be a push over and enable yourself to be harmed again and again. While you will relinquish any resentment that you may host against the gathering or gatherings that wronged you, you positively don't need to set yourself in a place for you to be harmed that way once more. It is impeccably adequate to be somewhat more careful now that you have seen what these individuals are able to do. Be that as it may if it's not too much trouble be exceptionally cautious. On account of minor offenses, which are those that were not deliberately noxious, don't wrongly assume that the demonstration speaks to who the individual is. If it's not too much trouble recall that we as a whole commit errors and we too have caused another person torment.

Tolerant is additionally not an open door for exact retribution. Proclaiming that you have tolerant somebody isn't a declaration that you currently have the "high ground." The people included may have been blameworthy, however, they absolutely don't owe you anything. Regardless of whether they don't apologize, you have still picked up a considerable amount by expanding this peace offering and relinquishing the sharpness that once devoured you. Keep in mind that by being tolerant, you are helping yourself out. While they may profit because of your choice, tolerant them is really a blessing to yourself.

The most effective method to Forgive

Since we are both mindful that generous somebody who hurt you isn't simple, I could never request that you do as such in a split second or at the same time. You have the alternative of excusing in stages. Step by step relinquishing your hatred towards the people who have wronged you will guarantee that you have enough time to find any hint of the sharpness you have towards them, insane and heart. In the event that you get the chance to see this individual regularly, you can begin by essentially making proper acquaintance.

This may come as an amazement to them since they were not expecting such a nice thought, and that may open the path for the exchange you both need to get some conclusion. Some of the time, despite the fact that you were wronged, it is best to step up with regards to set issues straight. Keep in mind forget how this modest demonstration will profit you over the long haul, regardless of whether they value the motion or not.

Another basic exercise that will assist us with forgiving is recording the name of the individual or people that hurt you and posting everything that they have ever done to agitate you. When you have finished that rundown, compose a rundown of the considerable number of events on which you have harmed somebody, and needed to request absolution. This isn't something that we are slanted to consider. Finding in high contrast how regularly we have given our unfortunate propensities a chance to hurt everyone around us, particularly those we cherish, might be only the push we have to relinquish any hard feelings we may have. What is significant all the more disturbing to a few people is the point at which they see the names of the individual they disdain on the rundown of people who they have needed to request tolerant.

Another valuable exercise is making a rundown of all the great things this individual has improved the situation you. This activity will assist you with remembering that in spite of their flaws, this individual or these people, have numerous lovely characteristics also. On account of those nearest to us, these characteristics are the simple motivation behind why we adored them and kept them shut in any case. Simply think, expressing the desire for peace of peace may even assist this individual in seeing the imperfection in their reasoning and improve. You would have improved the world a place by helping only one individual to improve as a man. Such thoughtfulness does not go unnoticed or without compensation.

It takes an exceptionally solid individual to excuse. Be that as it may, consider how much better our lives would be in the event that we didn't stroll around with the severity of hatred every day. Relinquishing that overwhelming weight is a standout amongst other approaches to recuperate ourselves. This world was at that point a fiasco, and it surely does not require any greater hatred to aggravate it. The following section will clarify how being tolerant can likewise enable us to end up far more joyful, and more effective individuals in this world, basically by being tolerant.

Section four - Be Friendly

Being friendly means being warm, obliging, delicate and agreeable. To get a companion, you should be a companion. Much more adage is the maxim, 'flying creatures of a plume, rush together.' If you need to pull in upbeat, strong individuals into your life, you should be that sort of individual. For what reason would anybody need to associate with you generally?

As the astute Maya Angelou featured, long after the memory of the association has blurred, individuals will recall how that communication influenced them to feel. When we are unfriendly, we make the lives of people around us considerably harder than it must be. We influence them to feel disliked, overlooked and separated when we are mean or upsetting.

OK like anybody to regard you as such? Okay, appreciate such unforgiving treatment? Wouldn't you say treating individuals that route at work, at school or in your own home, makes your life a considerable measure harder than it must be too? Consideration encourages a soul of participation, even among individuals who don't generally know each other. Encircle yourself with individuals who will work nearby you is far less demanding than endeavoring to vanquish this world alone.

Being unfriendly envelopes a wide assortment of activities. Our words are the most widely recognized type of unfriendly. Being cruel, stooping or even sudden, can be deciphered as unfriendly. Utilizing your words to put others down and hoist yourself isn't just unfriendly, it is likewise an extremely narrow-minded act, that regularly causes more damage than anything else. A key part of thoughtfulness is being respectful. Give us a chance to set aside some opportunity to take in more about this lovely quality.

For what reason Be Polite

Being polite is truly not as hard as a few people influence it to appear. While the facts demonstrate that being polite is ending up progressively troublesome because of the adverse states of mind of the general population around us, it isn't outlandish. Being polite may swell the personality of these people, however, our being polite is not a reflection on them.

Our being polite considers decidedly our character, no matter what. People who are polite are regularly thought of as friendly, principled, proficient and wonderful. What's more, with this exceptionally interconnected world that we live in, you just never know who you may have offended.

Simply envision how humiliated you will be in the event that you appear for a prospective employee meet-up, just to understand that the man you simply reviled in the parking area since you think they stopped in 'your' spot, is really the questioner. Trust me, it has happened ordinarily previously and could transpire.

Being polite includes being aware and chivalrous of the requirements, emotions, time, assets, values and social standards, of others. Being polite and friendly will make you exceptionally amiable and will urge others to respond your thought. Another advantage of being polite is that it will make it simple for you to pick up the regard of the people around you.

Regardless of whether they don't immediately change their conduct, they will be compelled to regard you and your measures. In the long run, they may improve because of your endeavors. Wouldn't life be substantially simpler on the off chance that we as a whole had occupations in which our representatives, subordinates, and partners, all approached us with deference? Regard must be earned and being polite is one of the most effortless approaches to win it.

Step by step instructions to be Polite and friendly

1- If you don't have anything friendly to state, don't state it, post it via web-based networking media or even think it. Indeed, even words that are whispered to a companion have been known to pivot and chomp you.

2- Don't be niggardly with welcome and greetings. In the event that you go into a room, agreeably welcome all present. When you are leaving, mercifully pardon yourself. Furthermore, on the off chance that you are welcomed, react warmly and with a grin.

3- Do not scrutinize the endeavors of others, particularly when clearly they made a decent attempt to achieve a specific assignment. In the event that you should offer some productive feedback, sandwich it with some certifiable honor.

4- Be energetic about the endeavors of others. Regardless of whether what is displayed isn't to your enjoying, there is no compelling reason to make it known.

5- Try to find out a little about the social standards and convictions of people around you. You don't need to share their perspectives, you just need to know enough not to unexpectedly annoy them. It is likewise most amenable to enable them to unreservedly express these perspectives, without dread of being slighted. You can simply settle on a truce.

6- You don't generally need to demand things being done your direction. Allow another person to sparkle once in a while.

7- Don't hoard discussions by talking just about yourself and your achievements. Show individual enthusiasm for others by getting some information about themselves and really tuning in to what they need to state.

8- When somebody is addressing you, give them your complete consideration. Quit strolling, composing or whatever else you are doing, and look. In the event that you are occupied, respectfully stop, assess how long the discussions should be, guarantee them that you esteem what they need to state, and after that mastermind a more appropriate time to proceed.

Section five - Be Truthful

The main thing more regrettable than a liar is a hoodlum. Liars make life troublesome and regularly don't understand the expansive impacts of their activities. Lying makes us troubled individuals, who continually must cover our tracks and watching our backs. Indeed, there are a couple of things as harmful as a liar. We ought to never enable the pessimism in this world to constrain us to end up unscrupulous individuals. Lying will just put you closer to the entryway that prompts duping and taking. Stop while you are ahead. Simply consider the conceivable results of a solitary demonstration of deceitfulness:

- Permanent harm to your notoriety

- Permanent harm to your connections

- Loss of pay

- Loss of dignity

- Permanently harming the notoriety of another person

- Feelings of blame

- Loss of rest

- Loss of trust

In the event that you examine the word truthful, you discover equivalent words, for example, respect, genuineness, reasonableness, respectability, uprightness, righteousness and honesty. Being truthful requires more than not lying when in a troublesome circumstance.

Being truthful requires being ethically upright no matter
what. At the end of the day, we will attempt to be honest
in every way and gain the trust of the people around us, by
methods for our activities. In any case, trustworthiness is
an exceptionally dubious thing. It is difficult to list every
one of the territories in which we should be truthful.

A decent general guideline on the off chance that you are
uncertain if a demonstration is truthful or not, is whether
you need to shroud it or delude somebody into trusting
you did something else. On the off chance that you should
stow away or cover your tracks in the wake of doing or
saying something, you are presumably not being
straightforward.

The advantages of being truthful far exceed any difficulties
you may see because of this course. Think about the
genuine feelings of serenity of not rethinking everything
you might do or viewing behind you since you are
continually in dread of being discovered. Envision
awakening and not being loaded by the overwhelming
blame because of your activities. What's more, don't be
tricked into believing that nobody profits by your
genuineness. It is anything but difficult to end up pulled in
to and to regard somebody who is straightforward. Most
bosses incorporate that quality as being absolutely critical
when looking for newcomers or thinking about a
conceivable advancement of somebody inside their
association.

Being truthful does not imply that we should volunteer the
majority of our private issues to everybody who is
attempting to pry into our business. Rather, we ought not

to withhold important data from people who merit an honest answer.

Being truthful likewise implies keeping away from the different implies that will fly up to get more than we merit or persuading something important to us that aren't valid. There are, in any case, times when a few of us may wind up in exceptionally disastrous circumstances since we are thought of as being excessively legitimate.

This is regularly the situation when our words are not tempered with graciousness. The following section will investigate how that property can enable us to stay away from a great deal of the issues that can result from that kind of discourse.

Section six - Know your own boundaries

A key part of the aftereffects of a Myers-Briggs Personality compose test is the segment which diagrams your qualities and shortcoming. A great deal of the mix-ups we make and issues we experience could have been kept away from out and out in the event that we were somewhat more learned about our boundaries. Simply consider an enthusiastic weightlifter who endeavors to lift excessively, too early. What might happen? Any reasonable individual will understand that the weightlifter will hurt themselves. Some will contend that this representation is urging us to boundaries ourselves, and in the event that we do, and quit propelling ourselves, we will never know our actual potential.

There are no boundaries to what you can accomplish on the off chance that you set your psyche to it, and some of the time you will never know how solid you are until the point when you attempt. You have to, in any case, guarantee that reason and rationale win when connecting with accomplishing your objectives. In the event that you have never lifted 100 pounds, perhaps beginning with 20 pounds today would be a superior thought. There is nothing amiss with preparing to stun the world, yet I would urge you to begin little and work your way up. Fundamentally, I am urging you to be unassuming in your desires.

Humility won't just assist you with avoiding setting impossible desires, it will likewise assist you with setting reasonable time allotments to accomplish your objectives. Numerous individuals end up disappointed when they achieve a specific age and have not accomplished a specific objective. In any case, simply think about the complexity between Mark Zuckerberg and Colonel Sanders. Check Zuckerberg established his Facebook domain in his mid twenty's, however, Colonel Sanders did not turn into the organizer of Kentucky Fried Chicken (KFC) until the point when he was in his eighty's. The two men are considered profoundly fruitful, however, each made progress at various occasions.

Possibly it's simply not your opportunity or perhaps you are only not in the correct business. As featured in section 1, picking a vocation in a field you adore, will assist you with staying roused and end up fruitful. This hypothesis is shown in the lives of both of these men. Their prosperity was because of an energy for something they cherished.

An unobtrusive way to deal with life will likewise assist you with avoiding contrasting your accomplishments with those of other individuals. A few people hit the ball out of the recreation center on the principal attempt, and there are other people who need to work their way up the stepping stool. Some will get hitched ideal out of school, others should hold up a couple of years and kiss a couple of frogs before they locate the correct individual. Truth be told, both Mark Zuckerberg and Colonel Sanders experienced numerous mishaps while in transit to progress. You will as well. Try not to expect that your life will be extraordinary. Regardless of what you would like to accomplish, you will need to work harder than you have ever worked previously, and you may need to hold up longer than you expected as well.

The delightful nature of humility stretches out a long ways past getting to be fruitful. This is a quality that will assist you with stopping taking on more than you can realistically handle. You don't have to state yes to everybody. This applies both to your own life, and at work. Try not to consent to preposterous due dates since you need to awe your manager, except if you are 100% certain you will have the capacity to finish the assignment. In the event that you have been given a task, and you are uncertain about how to complete it, don't be hesitant to request help. On the off chance that you work an all day work and have a family to deal with, don't focus on a lot at your youngster's school. Know thy boundaries! This applies to your chance, vitality, feelings, and aptitudes. Unobtrusiveness works as an inseparable unit with trustworthiness, the following section will clarify you can recuperate yourself and enhance your life by methods for this quality too.

Section seven - Know who you are

Knowing your identity is an exceptionally critical part of mending yourself. How might you stay away from a debacle on the off chance that you are just skimming through existence with no reasonable feeling of a big motivator for you, and what you decline to endure?

There is a motivation behind why the residential area young lady with enormous dreams, who gets to the huge city, regularly winds up in some hopeless and might I venture to state, trading off, circumstance.

Think too about the miserable Doctor who is just a Doctor since his folks concluded that he expected to wind up the principal Doctor in their family. Shouldn't something be said about the hen picked mom's kid who dates a young lady he can't stand since it fulfills his mom? These three have a great deal in like manner.

Their concern can be clarified in the familiar axiom that focuses out that in the event that we don't know where we are going, any street will be the correct one. What's more, even better, 'in the event that we don't remain for something, we will succumb to anything.' at the end of the day, on the off chance that we don't comprehend ourselves, this incorporates our expectations, dreams, and goals, it will be simple for pretty much anybody to push us into a choice we will lament for whatever is left of our lives. Living down a decision you lament, particularly in the event that you need to confront its outcomes once a day, will be one of the hardest things you have ever needed to do. Living with the weight of these decisions is a piece of the reason numerous individuals are so severe and unkind. This isn't the manner in which I need you to explore through your life.

When we set aside the opportunity to comprehend who we genuinely are, the complexities of our own identities, we will have the keys to open our actual potential. You can't turn into your best self on the off chance that you don't comprehend what that involves. When you comprehend yourself, you will probably wind up picking a profession that you adore. Furthermore, it is very simple to be enthusiastically headed to accomplish incredible things when you are seeking after a profession that you cherish.

Furthermore, when you are at the highest point of your amusement, you will search out the sort of accomplices and companions that will make you glad and along these lines draw out the best in you. They will comprehend the manner in which you think and may figure a similar way you do as well. These are the sort of individuals who won't snicker at your fantasies or be desirous of your prosperity. Being encompassed by adoring, steady individuals, will make you a kinder, more joyful and might I venture to state, more fruitful individual.

People, who have a profound comprehension of themselves, are regularly more unequivocal and idealistic. That is on the grounds that these people are in full control of their life decisions and they picked well. They will probably observe openings where others see difficulties. It likewise requires far less push to be beneficial when you appreciate what you do. Furthermore, the way that you make the most of your vocation will give you a focused edge and you won't rely upon the acclaim of others for inspiration. The fulfillment of a vocation well done will keep you pushing forward.

I realize that these may appear perfect conditions, where our decisions are not reliant on the wants of our family and where we are largely solid enough not to surrender to the weight they will put on us to settle on a specific choice. Yet, trust me, knowing and really understanding yourself will open ways to circumstances you would have never observed coming generally. It will be less demanding for you to face the weights around you when you know unquestionably what the correct choice for you will be. I am not urging you to shrug your duties of accommodating your family, I am urging you to comprehend your identity and be consistent with your identity constantly. You will be considerably more joyful therefore, and far simpler to love, when you are not conveying the overwhelming weight of a terrible choice around for whatever remains of your life.

Step by step instructions to get to Know Yourself

This is less demanding said than done, however it isn't inconceivable. You can begin with some goal appraisal. This does not mean just asking the general population around what they consider you. Your cooperations with them, regardless of whether negative or positive, will keep them from being as goal as you require them to be. A superior alternative would influence utilization of a legitimate identity to test. One of the prominent alternatives is the Myers-Briggs Personality compose test. This test will figure out which of the 16 identity sorts of this hypothesis best portrays your identity. It has picked up ubiquity as of late in light of the fact that its outcomes can be utilized to decide the earth you work best in and even how you communicate with the general population around you. In addition whether you like the outcomes or not they have a tendency to be shockingly exact.

Vocation fitness tests are another awesome choice. These are intended to enable you to comprehend your range of abilities better and how you can utilize these aptitudes to choose the correct profession. It is never past the point where it is possible to begin a vocation that you can love.

When you have a precisely thoroughly considered arrangement that will enable you to tend to your duties and still wander into a field that you cherish, take the plunge. It may be a case that cash is tight and you are as of now lashed for time and will most likely be unable to make a move at the present time. Be that as it may, I would urge you to keep setting yourself up. Continue realizing everything that you can about that vocation on the web or from the general population around you. That way, if the open door ought to emerge, you will be in a situation to take it.

When you have set aside the opportunity to find out about yourself, you may locate some messy clothing and shrouded scars that you most likely would have rather kept covered up. Shockingly, you have been wearing these scars each day in the manner in which you associate with everyone around you. These scars could have made you too delicate to express how you feel or excessively chilly, making it impossible to think about the sentiments of others. Since you can see yourself plainly, turn into the best form of yourself. Adore yourself. Or more all else, be consistent with yourself. Knowing your breaking points is another vital expertise to ace keeping in mind the end goal to explore through this insane world effectively. This will be talked about in the following section.

At the end:

I trust you have profited from this book. By advantage, I imply that I trust you have chosen to roll out some much need improvements.

Advancement might be moderate at first, however, you will never lament the choice to improve yourself. Each progression, regardless of how little, is a stage forward, and can accordingly properly be seen as an advancement.

The universe has a method for remunerating the positive qualities in us and helping us to locate the positive qualities in others.

At this point, you ought to have understood that the key to mending ourselves, and effectively exploring through the calamity of life, lies in our grasp. Except if we recognize our own deficiencies, and effectively work to attempt and enhance them, our lives will never improve.